Pigment and Fume

LAURA-GRAY STREET

Published in 2014 by
Salmon Poetry
Cliffs of Moher, County Clare, Ireland
Website: www.salmonpoetry.com
Email: info@salmonpoetry.com

ISBN 978-1-908836-76-2

COVER IMAGE: *"First Light" by Kathy Muehlemann – kathymuehlemann.com*
COVER DESIGN & TYPESETTING: *Siobhán Hutson*
Printed in Ireland by Sprint Print

for Kyle and Sydna

Contents

III. Goya's Dog

I. Crow Psalms

An Entangled Bank

—with Darwin and Thoreau

An entangled bank. It is interesting to contemplate
humid June on the skin like wet feathers

in Saran Wrap. Picking the sticky fabric (cotton
blends, polyester, vinyl) from my sweaty legs,

I have to strip myself like a quick jerk
of Band Aid or masking tape from the car seat.

Sun block, lotions, creams stew into an oil
slicking down arms and chest and forehead.

Innumerable little streams overlap and interlace,
one with another, exhibiting a sort of hybrid-, shall we say,

product. Few phenomena give me more delight
than that kind of money in the bank. You and I

are clothed with many kinds of trafficking.
And the world, oh, the world is rank

with early-bird specials twittering amongst
the tax cuts; insect repellents of all varieties

tizzying up the place, and erratic earthworms
thrashing like heavy-metal bangers at

the street curbs. It is interesting to contemplate
the way sand pours off our eroded slopes like lava,

pulled down over the headwaters like balaclavas.
Everyone stays focused on the cash flow, which takes

the forms of the laciniated and imbricated phalluses
of bureaucratic henchmen. Just think of brain coral,

of lung fish, of bowels and all kinds of excrements.
We contrive a system to transport our runoff

to the treatment plant, where it is treated, well, like shit
and excreted. Piped through entangled banks and spit

back into the watershed. In heavy rains, volume exceeds
capacity and overflows, by design—so interesting

to contemplate—into your neighborhood streams, rivers,
lakes, aquifers, wells. And not only stormwater but also

untreated human and industrial waste and debris,
all running blissfully together as one intoxicated

toxic stream, transformed, converted, wholly
baptized and foaming at the mouth,

like the born again in the parking lot yesterday,
who, bless his heart, collared me when afternoon

had hit its steamiest, when I was unsticking myself
from the car seat. Few phenomena give more delight.

But it's important to stay calm and enjoy the amenities.
There is no end to the heaps of liver, lights, and bowels.

True, what I say is somewhat excrementitious in character,
but isn't it interesting to contemplate the plain liquid idioms

undulating along the ripple marks on the river bottom,
age after age, stratum upon stratum. Even the godless,

and accountants, must recognize the stubborn beauty
of such waves, and how from so simple, so rudimentary

a beginning such hopelessly entangled forms
have been, and are being, brewed.

Doorstep Ecologist

But it should have fur and sun.

Shaking the fern fronds, the small dog windeth.
She stands, forepaws perched on wickerback,

peering for squirrels. What do you do
with the no-longer-husband in the son?

With the you in the daughter?
I'd like something beautiful here,

something profound, not this untuned
piano staining the wall.

Something exact, lineated,
scanning the low skies like aisles at the CVS,

as if birds were purchasable as envelopes.
There is bittersweet and ailanthus. There are herds

of white-tailed deer.
No mammalian tragedy for black comedy to pick clean.

The ancient Egyptians thought all vultures were female,
opening their vaginas in flight to the inseminating wind.

Thus translated "breeze scavenger."

Root tangle and stem, and the buzzards mathematical,
sine and cosine, pi in the sky, the sky a drawer of wing-nuts.

Except that's what you hate about Nature:
all those numbers, bleary, smeared, our trading on them.

I admit the disingenuousness of snow, rocks, birds, clouds.
And creeks, all bodies of water. But if a sentence isn't

a black snake, why syntax and all its
sinuous equations? Consider: Sylvia was saving

herself for marriage, but then there was *Art*
in the Age Of Mechanical Reproduction. So she lost it

in the back seat of the Eighties. He used a sandwich baggy
as a condom. Those were the days before Ziploc.

Forget rigor mortising, clutter of taxidermy.
Not eviscerated but visceral: road kill. Because

it's a hell of thing to move a dead horse (the equipment
is part trapeze, crane, tow truck—and very

expensive). Why not let it rot in the field?

Open season. Demolition.
Lo, the small dog curls into an ear.

Lumber and mortar and everything mortal.

Efflorescence with each bang of the dust mop.

First Lessons in Beekeeping

Walking into the humming,
he said to me, *Don't be afraid they
can smell your fear.*

I had long hair then, lank on my neck
and shoulders that were halter-bare
and glazed with summer sweat.

*

Sometimes the house swarms with bees. Finding no exit,
they console themselves with plaster, harvesting
dust in their pollen baskets. A household.

*

I was drawn to the boy blindly, circumstantially.
He kissed me between rows of tasseled corn.

Led me by the hand to the hill of bee hives.

*

Sometimes I feel them at my elbow, urging,
or browsing along femur, murmuring
through sternum, lodging
in inner ear.

*

Because all honey comes from bees.

*

The orange peels on the table steep
in afternoon light, staining the wood bitter,
dense flesh emptied to formality.

*Old bees they fly off and don't come back.
Fly out to die because flying out and dying is what they do.*

*

But reports of dead drones cascaded down the hives,
mats of dead bees pooled almost six feet around the hives.

And pollinators that live in hedge rows and woods:
feral, fading.

*

Electric air.

Don't run, he called
as I ran downhill, bucking,
as the bees tangled in my hair drove
their stingers into my scalp and neck.

*

You get enough Nosema cranae, *a colony will die.*
You get enough viruses, the colony will die.
You get enough mites, the colony will die.
Enough exposure to insecticides, enough drought,
enough sudden weather, enough sterile pollen,
enough stupid people, the colony will die.

*

Was it the shampoo—lab-constructed
supermarketed florals—that drew them
so deeply into that curtain?

Then the animal undercurrents—oily fear,
metallic adrenaline—bubbled up,
agitated the room.

*

Sometimes, balled as one body
they careen and swerve, launch
themselves at chinks and chippings,
probing for flaws. A muscular
frustration.

*

Orange seeds in my palm:

I imagine the groves now stranded,
pinpricks of bee hum and sun that burn
when I close my hand.

*

Hold still
Hold still Hold
still Hold still
Hold
still

*

When a bee lands where my hand's still
sticky with juice, I will myself to relax,
to breathe calmly and focus on observing this
infinitely interesting living thing.

*

No almonds, cherries, peaches, apples,
avocados, blueberries, cranberries, sunflowers,
cantaloupes, watermelon, cucumbers, oranges.

Only planks and dry wall.

*

Then I give way to instinct.

*

I can still taste that first kiss
of bees in my hair.

If I could have walked
calmly with them from there to here.

Maternal Pastorale

Morning: she wanders the field picking
buttercup and clover. Cows churn liquid jaws,

slow eyes revolving. An orb spider alert to
strands trembling with gnat, he feels the tug

of stems and comes looking. He finds her
and falters. How can he want a mother

—breasts seeping, belly stubborn, blunt
as a beast already burdened, already

at ease? Here is no hunger he can feed.
And her daughter, curled on the cord, still hipped

in membrane: premature. For now he'll pause,
admiring the bouquet, thoughtful connoisseur

who scents ripening, who relishes the complex body,
those hints of spectacular finish—then he'll leave

them placid, oblivious. A mother's thirst
he hasn't learned yet, how it can turn

fanged canines on the pursuer
and shred; how it runs with the maenads,

how she'll howl like the hell hounds themselves
as she drains the cultivated world, this

very field, down to backwash and sediment,
dregs of ice scum, weed husks, empty chitin.

Beggars

are branches scraping an empty metal bowl
at dawn—
are urchin birds sifting through bark
and brush, asphalt and gravel—
are raggwool-skeined hills unraveling—
are dove purling from a basket-weave
of pine—

are starved—until one cardinal
wells like a needle prick in the pecan tree.
That morsel of color, a hint
of blood, makes me say the pecan husks
still on the tree are winter flowers,
and the cedar is not dying
but variegated—

to say my uncle twitching through frowns
and grimaces of drugged sleep
is an infant, and his fingers, playing
invisible keys, are not calculating
—banker, Baptist, payment
in hard, cold cash—but reliving
his photographs:

hay field salted with frost; bluebirds
fresh-hatched and gaping; a box-turtle,
beaked in the satin red of a tomato—plush
as the inside of a coffin—
When are we not hungry?

To buzzards, the charitable road
gives dead possum for free—
raw wound scabbed in blood-black,
the ravenous birds now peeling off with
cleric's rustle, hinge's creak,

now settling in a tree, muttering *cure curate*
and eyeing me, the heresy who takes
but doesn't eat.

But you, my possum friend, what you see
is a mystery, and how it uses you
brilliantly. I steal back time
and again, fixing you
clearly, stain by stain, until your bones
are stripped of flesh and stench
and dragged away—
I say nothing
—*nothing, nothing*—
until the chant repudiates, flies
in the face of nothing so nothing the very

gasp is something
sharp, insistent, cunning—
something that gives us this day—
beggertick, burdock, cocklebur—
barb and spine stitched into shanks,
shoe lining, socks—
kneeling here in these curious
whispering weeds—
what makes fast keeps feeding—
hearing the buzzards curse—

O fanatic
may you blister—
Your shadow favors the inbred
emboldened worm,
the ingratiating fly,
and considers not
who cannot afford, unearned,
unearned ligament, tendon, intestine.

With our flight you purchased
meat that your eyes alone,

because they eat
dishonestly, steal outright.
We are stained by what we breathe
freely, but you,
by abstaining, contaminate.

Approximate, unclean
licker, finish and be off
that we may return
to the stench of friends
who feed us;

and after us, flies;
and after flies,

wind.

Walking the Train Trestle

The first steps
require a tourniquet
on the nerves, to
see you leaving
the diminutive
bluets and huge
red poppies, passing
from the shadows
of the hydroelectric
dam. But then you
are where each foot
lands, secure,
until the next step.
And if you watch
the wood only—
how solid the footing
over all that air.
You're taking the pulse
of distance. You're
growing splinters
and tar. Now you
untether to mud
and carbon spit,
a spark jumping
synapses of ties still
running sap. You're
arc-light of sudden
fish, an aluminum
flashing under
river skin, gone
too far for creosote
and screech to keep you
when tracks flood
dead-on with piston hiss

of tankers, hoppers,
boxcars hacking by, then
turning with the river,
fading west. This leap
of faith that leaves us
emptied, sieved of any
where or *how* or *what*
you are, the way colors
of galaxies of stars
are invisible, locked
in the calcified sky,
but still, yes, still as
immanent as the dam's
primary coil spinning,
an implacable,
placable hum behind
chain link and brick.

for S.C., 1982-2000

Potters' Field

*—a piece of ground reserved as a burial place for strangers
and the friendless poor*

             Then the storm
furls like a snapped sheet, folds neat
into the eastern drawer,

and it's an evening for sunset collectors,
we like to say.

Sky deepens
             from flush to muscadine
like the cherries, tree-ripened.

                      *Except where crows peck: pits dangle,
                      withered stars on black stems.*

Let us rehearse a lifetime's
opalescence:
             what we remember
folds straight-seamed with what we will;

             what we will,
that white cotton, wears smooth with cleaning.

                      *We remember the blood that ran
                      through the birds of our appendages.*

So we tease thread
through cloth until it gives

into another stitch. Rise and fall,
pucker and smooth.

Thread knotted
like a branch of forsythia; thread knotted
like the lilac or buddleia.

Our necessary scraps and buttons.

Only field stone and rotting log
mark our shed snake-skins, dull scales,
dark holes our mouths moved through.

But useless,
uprooting old losses. Let them lie,
numerous, anonymous,
as if they crept off this life when their shadows
shrank to toadstools at noon.

Even here, engrossed in the remains
of sun, barefoot, abstracted, disarrayed,
you won't see—
        We are the anthill's
erratic swarming at your instep. We are
the opportunistic weeds you pick:
bindweed, loosestrife, alyssum.
We are the ground wasps
burrowing chambers in your shade.

Catfish

Tossed stones
lodge in mud where

bottom feeders
lurk like grudges, trailing

tensile whiskers under
the surface. You hardly

see them they move
so deliberately, low

clouds, tarnished loaves
of pewter shadowing

the reflections of bare
trees capillaried in

sponge-gray sky. What
is the membrane gleam

a fetus sees on the brink
of being? Would it be

these first sun streaks
muddling the horizon,

the pond, the woman
on the shoreline who

wants and doesn't
care and even envies

what's there below
daylight—that

thick sediment
of slow fins? Who

wishes, stone
by stone, to be,

not the brimmed
bowl, but submerged,

not having yet
breathed in this

bridge of sighs.
Because to breathe is

to fall: it happens
only in air.

Ring-necks

Three hours she avoids the cock
and hen, flushed from the same rise, tucked
close as sleeping lovers, a delicacy

too touching to waste. Still the driveway
stays empty. Shushing the whimper
of the dog's linoleum-clicking dreams,

she lifts each bird by the neck and turns
to his penciled instructions. He'll have
some explaining to do. But no use

crying as blood jewels their beaks.
The quills she tugs sputter
like candles. Down drifts,

and the dog rouses its nose
to the smoky air. How brightly
wings snap at the shoulder, span

and retract. Flesh and breastbone
yield to knife-slice a handful
of curled intestines, plump

stomach, thumbpads of liver.
Flushed under tap the parsed guts
quiver; run clear. She plumbs

the cavity again, feels how firmly
the small heart roots before it gives
over to its leaded end.

She crouches; offers it on the flat
of her hand, the dog's warm tongue
sponging her open palm. That

moment she notes the presence of another,
smooth, indecipherable as a creek stone
—then it's gone.

Crow Psalms

1. Driving home—immobile clouds
   bank above a roadside
   of scrub brush, fence post, red earth

   spinning fast.
   Buzzards coast drafts—thugs
   that stroke such perfect turns—

   and crows scaffold on barbed wire.
   One crow won't budge from what's
   dead in the road . . .

   Not dead—held taut, clamped
   to the yellow line: a black snake,
   ditch-bound, its full length

   straining like a stalled engine
   to escape. Playing the accelerator
   against the clutch, I stay

   at a mesmerized idle
   in the middle of heat mirage
   and tar, all wheels still.

   And the crow: grim-beaked, wings spread,
   eyeing the car like a prospector
   gauging cost and profit

   —being, being fed—
   bets the odds
   on the course I'll take.

2. The crow scatters
    birds from the feeder
    in a gust of chickadees, titmice,
    wrens, then flaps off black
    as a loose eyelash, raucous
    as grit, *caa*, *caa* outside
    the unwashed window.
    The weight of a lone
    crow on the power line,
    its cockeyed
    scrutiny, makes us
    speak, hard pleas
    for subsistence—
                        Deliver us
    from our own—
                        Meanwhile
    October litters the yard.
    Apples slouch in frost that runs
    all scent to ground, the black walnut
    aims its loaded weapons,
    acorns scree the hills
    from under us—
                        Safer
    to watch out a window,
    scribbling in clouds of breath
    while crows ransack
    the pecan tree—

3. March and still the deadweight of winter
   muffles all with a heavy quilt. Broken snow.
   Shrub-shaped mounds. Sparrows skirting the edges
   of footprints. Six white inches float us
   above a surface we know only to a shovel's depth
   in spring.
            There: fat finial of crow bunched
   on the heaven-most spike of pin oak. As I pass,
   changing angles, the white-gloved sky
   palms the vertical twig and it disappears,
   and the motionless crow
   levitates.
            It's a trick
   of the eye, surely; crumbs thrown
   to the hungry—but who cares
   while the crow,
                    now tossing off
   like a top hat,
                    now unsleeving an endless
   black scarf,
                    laughs into thin air.

II. The Art of Navigation

Meet Me at the Speed of Light

Meet me at the speed of light, where mass
marries energy. I promise I'll be on time.

Music is math, and ribosomes play amino acids
note by note to compose proteins. There's a gene

that rules rhythm in a worm's life: eating,
excreting, laying eggs. An electron and a positron

collide in a bar. Both particles disappear.
Get it? I'm caught between the here and now.

I've come to this table with nothing but
piecemeal knowledge in my pockets.

Gambling on pulses of glands and orifices.
A few more read and a few more shed.

One can't remain forever in a state of paroxysm.
The Brain Institute wants molecular control

of your behavior. Talking to God is a habit,
running our mouths the way a toilet runs.

See how quickly the tables turn? Indoor
plumbing was our real estrangement

from the weather. It's a sore spot
where you put your finger. Don't hold back.

Primate Center, Duke University

In their native Madagascar, aye-aye are considered bad luck, and
villagers hunt them down whenever possible. Legend has it that if
an aye-aye points its bony third finger at you, you will die soon.
                                        SCIENCE NEWS, *Apr. 1992*

An aye-aye, one of the world's least-known primates and among
its strangest, clung to a coconut frond three feet away. [. . . T]he
aye-aye stared at him for a few minutes, as if curious about a fel-
low primate, before nonchalantly disappearing back into the night.
                                        BIOSCIENCE, *Nov. 1993*

1.

The guide shushes us at the edge. Beyond
fluorescence, the simulated night stirs;
calibrates a prosimian ear; draws near.

A long index finger, toothpick bone,
wanders—with an ant antenna's deliberate
tap, or an inchworm's nudging measure—

a scruff of coconut. And when the aye-aye
finds the nut's fontanel, the soft eye,
he bores a hole to extract the insides.

He peers at us from the dark. We're
gripped in silence as he spoons up finger-full
by finger-full until—intact, hollow-skulled—

the dropped husk's thud breaks the spell.
We blink; stretch—emergent, peripheral—
What light originates—

2.

What light originates at this center
troubles our most rational
irrational selves, and our jigsawed

dreams are not clean of history.
At night, what startles us awake
is the wrong of a wrong number.

Test or accident? And by day, which
of the million pieces we squint over
will we find mis-stamped,

or missing? The matter of fact
is hard shell, dry seeds,
no possibility of meat or milk.

If you pick it up and shake it,
you can hear the organ
grind, and dance to the little bells.

Matriarch

In Paris she can-canned
without panties.
                Summers
she swam naked in the Atlantic
and smoked a pipe.
              For a pet
she kept a diamond she named
Big Boy; it wagged her finger
when it was happy.
              When
she was happy, she fed us
shots of vodka and opera, packs
of Blackjack from her golf closet.
We pocketed the wages
of her pleasure.
              Augusts,
we marched the sands: heads up,
shoulders back, skin tight, tight
in string bikinis—nylon
hot as a tongue—
              because the girl
she was walked barefoot over coals
when they'd dared her, her soles
too seared to ever feel again
what was beneath her.
              The day
we caught her napping with a book
of matches, she let us adore her heels
with the glowing tips, a burnt
offering—incense of sulfur, ash,
and flesh—that's kept us young
as moths ever since.

The Art of Navigation

He set black and white on fire.
HARRY GAUGH ON FRANZ KLINE

The rugged brushstroke of the dying oak
is left standing for a week, limbless

as the marriage we find ourselves
dismantling. Without leaves

or branches to create perspective,
trunk and sky, shape and space, equilibrate

in the same plane, a balance of black
on white, white on black,

like the sketch Franz Kline enlarged,
in 1949, on a Bell-Optican projector,

crosscut of a junk-shop wooden rocker
he loved to paint as much as he loved

and painted his wife Elizabeth, Elizabeth
already lost then in her dark refrain.

When he saw himself in a book
she gave him—Nijinsky as Petrouchka—

Franz painted that face to its grave. Over
and again he laid the dancer down, poor

swallowed soul, cheeks pinched hollow,
bent head pinioned by harlequined

hatband, lidless eyes eyeing nothing
but his own foreshortened depths.

Years of tracing, retracing steps
until the facts of the matter distilled

to stark architecture, passionately
unconcerned with finish—

Elizabeth, Elizabeth—
the same dark refrain—

But today the tree crew returns
to finish the job. One shimmies

up rope to test what's solid or void, and log
the byproduct for winter. Now he shouts

he's found monarchs, just a small clump
high on the bare trunk, resting up,

absorbing the sun's heat: this time of year
they route their way by warmth—

Some paths depend on abstraction
(the blind foraging of sleeping backs

until the spines meet, hinge into wings).
Who knows how invisible lines

line the visible better than an old
sight-gagged clown? So teach, you paint-

and-pain-masked mime. I can't find my way
any other way. Teach me to read maps

in the cadmium and singe-veined flakes
of monarchs brush-fired and dispersed

on a breeze, in the tree that
with the lightest of gestures,

like a finger touched against flesh,
the chainsaw opens, ring after ring.

—*in memory of Larry Levis*

Lares et Penates

The arsoned warehouse still smolders—
black brick, jagged timbers, all glass
scorched away. What remains,

surviving use, are three arches—
Flemish bond, surprisingly ornate—
cupping flickers of leftover flame.

Last night's trucks, hoses, firefighters
scrambling have flattened surrounding
scrub brush the way a lover once said

sex splays a woman's pubic hair.
He told me that after sex, *a woman
is a burnt-out building*. He said this

affectionately, as an endearment,
If you ask me, *What kind of man—?*
I'd say a good one. Good

as the hot tip one mother used
to imprint caution on a child caught
lighting matches, on the palm

of her child's uncalloused hand.
Good as a warm body turned to
in an anonymous, unrecorded dark

and brisk departure. That comfort:
flash of nerve and muscle cauterizing
a greater, more prolonged loss (a long

tending, feeding desire from the inside)
with a sense of—what? Accomplishment?
The arch, Leonardo said, *is nothing else*

than a force originated by two
weaknesses. This is *architecture*:
arch. Root sense: "built like an arched

brick oven." Then with sense shift:
"the arched construction of a brick oven."
L. *fornus, fornax*, oven (FURNACE).

Because Romans used the arched brickwork
under buildings, and because the prostitutes
of Rome lived in these underground hubs,

early Christian writers evolved the verb
fornicari: "to frequent brothels." The whores
of Pompeii fornicated in similar stone cribs.

Drawn by fire, a crowd now gathers along orange
security tape. Suddenly the day feels intimate,
the way we shift side to side, stamping our feet;

the way we steam like animals of the field,
a thermal correspondence that would ease us
but for the thumb-tight fists we blow through

with visible breath. This breath—do you see?
—this smoke from the hidden fires we light
and, sometimes bare-handed, extinguish?

To shape the Roman arch, Vitruvius
needed concrete: lime and water
mixed with *pozzolana*, which is

Vesuvian ash, pebble and grit. *When
these substances, all formed by fire,
are mixed, the water taken in makes them*

cohere, and quickly hardens them—
In 1864, excavating Pompeii, Giuseppe
Fiorelli discovered how ash had hardened

so closely around corpses that, decomposed,
their exact contours were preserved.
Into these hollows, he blew liquid plaster,

which solidified. *Above all an arch*
is a mechanism of transit and transition,
dividing two areas without sealing off either,

inviting passage, suggesting a place beyond
different from that within. All the while
our sun moves west; continents drift

on warps of Archean rock, fact after
fact hardening into artifact. —The night
a man died on the sidewalk, you drove

air through his flaccid lungs and broke
ribs to punch his failing heart.
I lost him, you said, stripping off

vomit and sweat. I collected clothes
you trailed to the bathroom, nosing
your shirt for a concrete shape for loss,

losing you behind a curtain of steam.
How could I tell you water won't ease
the scald of one mouth on another?

What remains is this: your gray eyes
on my eyes, your drenched beard
on my skin, our skin flushed

over bones surprisingly ornate.

Phosphenes and Entopics

Once there was a ceramicist who cast
vessels the size of human beings.

Asked why he punctured each new jar
by striking the soft clay with a two-by-four,

he closed his eyes and answered,
"To let the darkness out."

Recreation Center

This is the boy who calls it *nigger dog* and kicks hard
at its tobacco-yellow ribs. This is the woman, just a volunteer,
who looks and looks away. This is the bone crack you can't hear
with so many kids yelling. This is what you hear—
this is shut yo watch this ain't naw you it—

This is the tobacco the boy packs hard; the cigarette
he sucks down to nub and flicks at a crack in the asphalt.
It lands beside the dog under the sliding board.
This is what you see when you close your eyes.

This is a test. Now the dog, leg crushed, dragging
its whip-thin tail, wheezing on its haunches. Now the boy,
sliding his eyes at her—*White lady, you like this mutt?*
He whips the dog around by the tail, squeezes its muzzle hard, harder
until it whistles through its lip flaps. All the while eyeing him
eyeing her eyeing you. This is the thin music that uproots us.

Damn clean as a whistle—She taking his lip. These are
the little girls she'd save if she could, muses of the patrol car,
skinny as roots, the red and blue lights they love licking their faces,
their arms, their legs. (There is a girl the boy saves candy for
and then the condemned crawlspace she plays in
collapses. This is how he finds her).

These are the dog days of summer.
This is why the woman says, *Hey you boy*—then gasps:
because the dog whines to play when the boy calls *Here mutt—*,
and doesn't cringe at his outstretched hand. This is the last straw.
This is what we get. Is this what we've been waiting for?
Is this what we're afraid of? Is this seat taken?
Is this what it takes? (*What it is what it is?*)

This is a crawlspace/ our last resort/ just the beginning/
how we play (fill in the blank). Tell me, what is the meaning
of this? These are ears pitched higher than human hearing.
This is the way to retrieve a broken body. This is why we're here,
isn't it? *This is* is an expletive; it should be deleted.

This is hard. This is the end. That
was once upon a time. This will be continued.
This is just to say. These are words (this is a *boy*, a *nigger*,
a *dog*). This is what dogs don't know:
why we cringe at a word as if it kicked (this is *fear*, this is *human*),
not hearing (is *just a woman*, a *girl* (—*his* girl, gone))
how a word looks ((away)).

The Way War Ends

Dilapidated, meaning coming
apart stone by stone and fully
alone. Knot of frayed blue plastic
vining a dead limb. Spittle
of geranium specking the open door.
Bridge slung bank to bank, a clang
of axel and gear shift. Downriver,
a storm plants itself in fields of sun-
flower, nuclear reactor, corn. This
is the way war ends, curling at the edges
like a smirk of old paper, a snarl. My
son grown strong armed in the ways
of fuses and fusion and wires. Halt,
who goes there, don't mess with these
crossed swords. This is the time
to call a halt, a ceasefire, bury
the hatchet, old friend. Stop flinting
flake by flake from the rock pile
while sooty curses fall softly
on us all. Clear the rubble, wade

into the aftermath and, glove

and boot, start heaving the residue.

Sure, it's sweaty work, as we

knew it would be, troops pulled out,

slumped in fatigue on the back

of flat-bed trucks. We crave sleep,

that deep genre poured over

the sluiceway. Instead, what's

ever cast out and hauled back

as hydraulic drowse and surface

to morning's mustard smear is

rough-shod wake up. The same

old quest for answers, the way

a dog embarks and barks and early

commerce growls its gears. My

son in uniform and saying

a hesitant goodbye. What isn't

now stone by stone coming apart.

Crowd Looking at a Tied-Up Object

chalk, pen, wash, and watercolor
HENRY MOORE, 1942

We can't imagine what's under the knots and drapes
cross-tied and Grecian in their folds something ancient
without arms or head a naked torso we've seen such things
in Europe— It could be a bomb or divorce famine war
a disease incurable and inexorable— I'm concerned
that we've walked so far our town a smudge of dry moss—
How could we leave the children, abandoning them

to their own devices— Someone should tell the others
a new commandment a revelation a harbinger a sign—
Do you know how much I want you let's slip away
who would notice— A random occurrence a new breed
a guiding principle— We could lie down in the shadow
of that boulder the one that curves like a boat a bone—
It's the most beautiful thing I've ever seen it comforts me

arouses me makes me want to hide— This is a desolate
place I am comforted by the presence of my fellow citizens
someone should make a speech this momentous occasion—
We must leave here before it's too late— An inspiration
an insult a fatal flaw a guilty conscience a commodity a gift
from God— I can't see that far without my glasses are you sure
they're not in your pocket— Last night I dreamed we walked

beside a lake the vegetation rose into a bear it ambled
toward us with what intent we couldn't determine—
I remember the last present my father gave me he handed it
to me saying "Son"— Remind me when we get back
to call my sister we spoke harsh words last we met—
A monument to the dead a testimonial to the unborn—
The first time I undressed you I trembled lifting off layers

fragile as shale— How can you not know that I love you
you can't want this to continue— My feet are blistered
I hear a faint ticking— You hear sand blowing or beetles
clicking in their tunnels they emerge each evening
when the sun is almost down— I'm so parched so thirsty—
Always you complain and moan— What becomes of the body—
What of the body— Please please stop mocking me—

We eased down the embankment the bear paused
cocked its head slightly but precisely in our direction—
I want to go but there's no room to turn I'm pinned
jostled forced to stand and look— How can I not follow you
to be near you love breathing in your breath— At dusk
we as crowd and object are reduced to clump and appendage
huddle and bound scurry and monolith regret and premonition—

The sum of all our emptiness the form— A pillar a cradle an ear—
Entwined we'll make a bigger body to dissuade the bear or die
together— The fates the gods the furies the spirits that guide us
protect us laugh at us deceive us— Why are we waiting here—
The enormity a mockery a blot a trial a transgression a stain—
We think we know what is coming we have no idea— Such
solid space around this hollowness— It follows us everywhere—

Harmonicas

I warn you that on the road to truth lurks many a dragon
and goblin of mischief in wait for the soul.

W.B. YEATS

On a branch two buzzards
mirror each other,
their wings outstretched,
drying dew in the wind

perhaps. Or they're courting.
For hours, arguing
the silent strain, like heavy
black wool on the shoulders.

I should go somewhere
and look for meaning
that way. Weight,
the way of testing the true,

the durable world . . .
A man with harmonicas
once joined my table
on break between sets—

show tunes, a round of gospel
to prove he was saved.
Or so he told me, placing
a one-hundred dollar

wood body in my left hand,
an eight-hundred dollar
steel body in my right.
"Weigh the music," he said,

"the relative values of sound."
That easily we should know
bad from good, good
from great. Not the years

of instruments the man
explained he threw away
before learning
to file his reeds and test

music with a meter,
matching, face to face,
note to true note. Then
he told me a joke—*the*

jim said to the spic—
that proved he was human.
"That's bad," I said,
needing a moral; adding,

"I met God once,
while I was running.
Near home, I heard him
snarling: *Runner!*

Run faster little girl—
Runner! I recognized
his long knotted hair
and beard; his defecations

in the yard; his bulk hitched
against a rusty camper,"
I said, measuring steel
against wood, "The neighbor-

hood schizo, drunk; off his
meds. I ran faster, his wind
at my back." "Back when,

I'd play and they all

came to hear me. Paid
good money too,"
the man with harmonicas
said, meaning more

than the bar's bad lighting
could disguise, or his
back-to-business riff
when he saw I couldn't

care less . . .
If we should meet
again—you and I, I
and you—spare me

this, against your better
judgment: light good enough
for shadows; wind to run on;
and the counterpoise to rest

my arms on the ledge
and watch the buzzards
finally folding, two

overcoats shrugged onto pegs.

The Brücke Choir

It's not what they are singing but that they are singing.
—from a comment on Georg Baselitz's painting *The Brücke Choir*

In the museum the young girl swung her mother's long-handled purse.
The docent gasped as she cyclconed toward Art. Toward something
photo-realist, I remember—a kitchen sink full of gleaming, foodless dishes.

Photo-realism relies on shine—chrome edges, curves of faucets,
cars and counters. Surfaces that catch the light the way wanting
makes us catch our breath. Your hand along the polished railing

of my hip. A photograph on an adjacent wall showed another kitchen,
Eudora Welty's: her table lined with jars of preserves and honey, tins
of tea and sugar, an aluminum ice tray, fringed curtains, linoleum.

Yellowed light sifts like talcum, but it's deceptive. Beside her window
something is plugged into the socket, but that something is outside
the picture, and the cord is naked as flesh between garter and stocking:

snapshot of skin an old lady tucks between wash-worn, practical garments.
I scrub my kitchen sink, wash the cloudy glasses, turn them mouth-down
to dry in the drain board. Out the window the nuthatch feeds bottom-up,

beak drilling the pine for insects. I know a man and woman who share blood
and lust—a libretto of restraint. They like to bone fish in the ocean.
Once, the boat reeled off shoals into surf. She would've fallen overboard

but he held her across the chest. Picture the tongues of her nipples
through wet cotton, the black hairs on his arm wired to each chill bump,
the tails of the vertically-feeding bonefish trilling along the surface,

the unswimmable current. Later, in the kitchen, cleaning and cooking fish,
the fork tines lifting the xylophone of bones from the steaming flesh.
They stopped at this, just as the girl in the museum stopped, so the docent

could breathe safely again. But we play these stops.
Today you drop into my kitchen and catch me wide-mouthed
in the act of singing. I believe too much in drowning.

A curtain of sunlight across the window.
The guttural faucet, a full-force choir.
The aluminum music sucked through the unstopped sink.

III. Goya's Dog

Breaking and Entering

Mornings she's pinned to her bed, fascinated
by utterances newborn and exotic as fuchsia horns
of bougainvillea: her mother, showering, singing
and speaking in tongues. At thirteen, she prays
for that gift as though she's raiding her mother's
makeup or fishing the tea-stained lemon
from her glass and touching it to her own tongue.
Being saved means finding God, or being found,
the way two sleeping parents can wind so
close their bedclothes enunciate only one,
the quilt sloping from their still form
like a hushed, moonlit lawn. She's no stranger

to miracles. She's seen people slain
by the Spirit, seized by the gift of prophecy,
healed by the laying on of hands. So why is she
surprised, baby sitting, kneeling at the sofa
on a sun-spotted oriental rug, when her prayer grows
incomprehensible? In that opulence, a twist of vowels
like smoke, and her throat taut, soft as a new leaf
embossed on damask, all wonder in her weaving
rich cloth, climbing the way a vine grows
toward what it isn't. Then the baby wakes crying
in his own opaque language. The moment opens
and closes quietly as a mother at the door. Or

the child she was, stopped short at her parents'
door by the luminous undulation of sheets,
their nocturnal blooming. Replaying that moment,
she keeps turning toward and away, entangled—
though *abandoned* is still just the cottage
she studies each summer, frame sinking
into itself, clapboard rinsed gray, shredded
to lattice, that one hot day they break in—

her mother and she—through honeysuckle
knotted over cracked windowpanes.
Like thieves they enter that place
where a man shot his wife as she slept

with another man. Unhinged cupboards,
rusted tin cans, dim sag of a hallway.
On the gap-planked floor, they find dust
surprised by their footsteps, and death
starker than any rumor: hundreds of bees
littering the bedroom like burnt bread crumbs.
They won't tread on graves, so they cut
pine-bough brooms with a kitchen knife
and turn—who knows why?—to sweeping.
Then they bless the mounded bodies, standing
arm in arm, tonguing citrus sweat off their upper
lips, rapt—as if they've merged and can lift

one wild trumpet from the vine and sound it.

After I'm Treated for Vertigo, My Daughter and I Eat a Pear

That our balance depends so much on these tiny pebbles—
calcium crystals sifting in our inner ears—makes me hungry

for the grainy texture of pear, so my daughter quarter-slices
the fruit and hands me two, telling me that what I'm craving is

sclerenchyma, a kind of dead plant cell that adds that special
something to pear and creates the structure that holds

all plants upright, which makes an odd sense, she says,
given the situation. I like how the nicknames—"ear rocks"

for the crystals; "stone cells" for the grit of pears—are tilted,
off-balance as slant rhymes. This morning I couldn't walk

a straight line to get the trashcan to the curb, and if this
continues, the neighbors will think I've started drinking.

See, my crystals have leaked into my inner canals, where
they scrape against my cilia and spin me in a centrifuge

until I'm clamped by an imaginary gravitational pull
to the bed or a chair or, right now, the floor—then keep me

knocked off kilter so that I'm all day wobbling on my axis.
And, dude, I say, I'm not even kidding. Better to stay here

in the kitchen, warm stone underfoot, my daughter sitting
in the doorframe she used to shimmy up like her fingers

and toes had suction cups when she was eight. Now
she's eighteen and we're sharing a pear while we talk

like *she's* the adult. As if that isn't cause enough
for vertigo. Which I now know isn't a fear of heights

but the sense that everything around me is spinning
out of my control. Think of reaching into a top shelf you

can't see and feeling something under your hand
jump and scuttle off. Or drowsing in sun and lurching

up from the chaise when a shadow falls on your face
as though someone's thrown you a ball. The way time

and space career. The way this kitchen smears as if it
can't catch up to my daughter's fingers, which still have

the tensile strength of guy wires when she collects our
gnawed cores and pitches them into the compost bin

like she's telling a good story, saying *Did you get more
pears?* and *I wish you would have* when I say no. Then she's

out the door. I'm breathing in the maculate hum. That's
how vertigo—this *now*—is abrupt and humid and mesmerizing.

Endosymbiosis

It's the same old song:
—*You're late.* —*You're awake.*

—*I couldn't sleep.*
—*Meeting ran long.* —*You should have*

called. —*The sky is clear tonight;*
I saw a few stars.

—*What on earth does it matter to me?*—
Endlessly, endlessly. The familiar

diorama. Binary stars, clenched
orbits. Now shaking each other off,

refusing to talk.
                Outside, taxis honk out
expletives. A wind with caffeine jitters

picks streetwise through litter.
Two seasons collide like passersby

hunched into pockets,
                intent on their business.
The self-absorbed minds gone tone deaf,

sullen, illiterate, blind, unmindful,
lost in crowds, litter, smog,

the necessary words unheard—
Skin-rimmed, oblivious of two

billion years archived in our intestines,
arguing life and love and death,

talking and talking since we gathered
enough of ourselves as a species

to speak. While the sea
we thought was cold,

bleeds. The air—empty—
breathes.
It's hard, this incessant

wading through membrane
after membrane. How fragile the broken

webs in our wake, each moment
trailing threads of rooms we

entered without listening.

Hôang-Tsong (The Yellow Bell)

In one version of the story, there are no birds,
only the man and his inventions. In another version,

the birds are phoenixes, dispensing heaven's
supreme wisdom. Then there is a third version.

In the stories of a story, there is always a path
between two sides, a middle way that is often true.

*

*North of the Kwen-lun Mountains, where the bamboo
grew to identical heights, Ling-lun cut a section*

*with his knife and blew. Nearby were two birds.
The first, wishing to imitate the singing bamboo, sang*

*six notes. The second bird, beginning from the last note,
sang six more. To imitate the birds, Ling-lun cut*

*eleven more bamboo shoots of different lengths. What
Ling-lun would take back to the emperor was new*

*and sturdy as a ladder. Together, birds and human
build the twelve semi-tones of the chromatic scale.*

*

Like most tales of how and why, this is a story
for children. *What time of year? What kind of weather?*

Do you remember hiding in the bamboo forest,
deep in the black labyrinth of paths,

crouching among beer cans, used condoms,
and urine stink until the game was over

and everyone had gone? The hush then
at twilight, birds and leaves indistinguishable?

Day after day. All summer. Do you remember
what you sang to yourself to keep so still?

*

The tube of Ling-lun's first note, the Yellow Bell,
is eighty-one inches. Divided into nine equal parts

of nine inches each, it established the musical foot
and the Chinese system of weights and measures.

Hôang is the yellow of soil, and the imperial color.
Tsong is the sound of two stones struck together.

Together, *Hôang-tsong* is the fundamental tone of nature.
It guides the emperor, the stars, the twelve-toned years.

This we can all hear, if we know how to listen.
The pitch of a voice speaking without passion.

*

In this story, your children hide in a bamboo thicket.
It's a game they like to play. They call,

and you must imitate. You are bird-footed. Your hands
are useless as wings. The thicket isn't large.

It stretches as far as you can see. With a mouthful of clay
and two stones, you must find a song.

*

Whether the stories are true or not,
you want to believe the sound of everything.

What will you tell your children before you die?
You must practice playing scales. Thaw crack.

Rustle of leaves. Stirring of insects. Rain
and murmur of flowing waters. Clear light.

Ears of corn and bearded wheat. Wind. Clouds.
Stars. Tangled green that wilts with cold snap.

The burrowed animals laying themselves down
to sleep. Intricate hoarfrost. The forming of ice.

Snowfall, first a little, then a lot—

Mozart's Starling in Central Park

One pigeon, foot drawn up, clenched to its belly,
a long stick bound to it in a tangle of filament
(the way I carry you in me). Where the stick

protrudes, the pigeon lacks a toe.
Maybe, caught on a branch a fisher hooked
and lost a line to, struggling to break free,

the bird shed its toe and gained this wood
(layers of pleasure on layers of pain),
and the wound closed over. Approach,

and the bird hops one-legged beyond reach
(the way I carry you in me). We speculate
that removing the stick would hurt more

than the original amputation, the bird's prosthetic
now intrinsic to balance (layers of pleasure
on layers of pain). Some viruses embedded

in ancient cells became necessary to,
finally indistinguishable from those cells,
until electron microscopes revealed trace borders

and property lines, aboriginal remnants unearthed
in metropolitan building sites. (The way I carry
you in me, layers of pleasure on layers of pain.

I've learned to hold my tongue.)
In the 19th century, Eugene Shiffelin released
in Central Park every bird named in the works

of Shakespeare. One box unleashed a horde
of *Sturnus vulgaris*: opportunistic invaders,
songbirds' bane. But even starlings I hear have

something to recommend them (I've learned
to hold my tongue). A starling displayed
at a Viennese pet shop sang the theme

from Mozart's Piano Concerto in G major, K. 453.
"*Das war schön!*" the composer exclaimed. He
carried the bird home (the way I carry you in me),

noting date, purchase price, and whistled fragment
in his expense book (I've learned to hold my tongue).
When it died, he buried his *lieber Narr*

with the pomp and mourning we accord
our own species (layers of pleasure
on layers of pain). Despite our efforts,

the pigeon maneuvers past trespass or remedy,
glides with its cumbersome appendage
(the way I carry you in me), to the rocks

by the lake a riveting gesture (layers of pleasure)
of immaculate balance (on layers of pain). (I've
learned to hold my tongue.) "That was beautiful!"

we gasp, wrenching ourselves free.

Cardinals

When the nest is empty, I figure cats or
the downpour finished them. But later

I see them in the holly, three fledglings,
wobbling from branch to branch in erratic

flits and bursts, then pausing, first pin
feathers trembling in the open air like ash,

like puffs of seed head on the verge.
They haven't grown into their beaks yet;

those oversized yellow grimaces seem
wired into place, so they wear masks of

fixed certainty as they negotiate precarious
stems. When they flag, their parents swoop

in, regurgitating insect mash into each
gaping mouth, and then hover, chipping

and cajoling the chicks into the oak tree
and over into the neighbor's Fortuna hedge.

Two of the three chicks make it across—
their bits of flight growing bolder, less

wobbled in aim—and blur into dusk
and tangle. The third fledgling is

still insistent in the holly. Fed, it then
tucks its head under wing and doesn't

budge. I'd worry, but the phone rings and
my own children need tending. I've taken

too much time here. Dandelion taproots
twist too deep to pull. They're hungry too.

On the Ladder

Bucket of apples: beads on an abacus:
counting on balance that's delicate, visible—

If this ladder slips like a book you'd drop
nodding off, simply catch yourself and stay:

the way muttering clay fists on rotted walnuts
and rhizomes of iris, and the garden hose loops

a ledge in precarious script: the way the jarred
widow spider broods over geometry; see her

hourglass tip on the fencepost without spilling
one stitch: the way the mockingbird—still—

circumnavigates a crow past its nest tree.
But gravity encourages us to fall down,

and even a buzzard staggers when it lands
on a dead branch that snaps and falls away

with a rattle, like the tool shed unlatched
to the dark of potting soil and mulch where,

early, a snake carcass raked from the eaves
uttered, out of its belly, the skeleton

of a bird. What you heard there
stays with you, weighs on you now

the way the ball of your left foot
relegates the sum of your whole life

to hollow aluminum. Still, there are
apples to pick. The ladder sways

as you plant your right heel on a sigh
of a branch and step out, trusting

the durable bones; depending,
as we must, on the steady breath

of trees, on the innumerable
raw and rare materials that bear

our figures of speech.

Goya's Dog

1.

Particle dog.
Dot on the horizon.
Paddling for all she's worth
Into the oncoming wave,
Into material, into density.
Out of velocity.
Into position.

2.

The black dog on the creek bank tracks a smudge of deer dashing
through deep woods. The squirrels are so enthralled in their spring
frisking they're oblivious to the dog, muscles tensed, nose quivering,
all her intricately-tuned-ballistic-system senses now locked in on
those luscious twitching tails. She dives into the ravine after them,
paws digging into the yellow clay heavy from recent rains, kicking
up the scent of lichen, log pile, and leaf rot, and in a single brushstroke
scattering the squirrels up trees and out of reach. The air is golden
because the light is golden and up is lighter than down.

3.

Go into your yellow, we are told, and so we do,
Easeled to a view of sunflower fields fronting the nuclear cooling towers.
The painter squints at my efforts and says,
This black splotch here looks like the head of a dog.
Heat looms like a car too fast around a bend.
We work like dogs panting in the sun, brushes in hand.
Like the universe expanding from the first hot bubble.
We want to know, we said.

4.

Because on their first and blind date in 1957, my mother is wedged up against my father who is driving the whole gang on this joy ride. She's trying to study for her final biology exam. The notes in her lap are diagrams of the male reproductive system.

5.

A law of nature has been broken
In a laboratory on Long Island
In a quark-gluon plasma soup
For a millionth of a billionth of a billionth of a second.
When gold nuclei travelling at 99.999% of the speed of light smashed together,
Up quarks moved with magnetic field lines; down quarks traveled against.
A break in parity, symmetry.
Maybe this can tell us why we're matter more than antimatter.
Why we matter.

6.

Because fifty years later, my mother sits with my father in the urologist's office, looking at the same diagrams of the male reproductive system while the doctor explains prognosis, treatment, progressions. And after the bladder is removed, chemo, radiation. And then maybe.

7.

Maybe the dog is an up quark.
Maybe the dog is a down quark.
Maybe the dog is in the soup.

8.

One day years ago, walking with the dog. Not my dog, my father's dog. A dog named Man. A golden yellow dog bounding in and out of golden rod along the country road.

9.

Then, a car coming too fast around the lonesome bend. After the collision, my father closing the window of the dog's eye; shoveling a hole in the field. That break in symmetry. The heaving of his shoulders. Still.

10.

Because the world is made of atoms,
Because symmetry underlies the laws of the universe,
Because the universe is expanding,
We count on the universe being neither right- nor left-handed,
On being even-handed, balanced, fair.
But the weak force of nuclear radioactivity
Isn't balanced. We've known this since the fifties.
Who knows where we'd be if we didn't
Matter more than antimatter.

11.

Around the bend, the black dog finds a possum carcass—putrid lump of bone and gristle and tissue—and gives herself to it utterly, bending her front left leg and lowering her shoulder, the way we'd ease into a hot bath. Then she's fully down and on her back, twisting her torso to and fro to rub it in, to embed the stink deep in her hair and skin. She's painted herself for us, grotto and gutter, pigment and fume.

12.

Wiping the brush on a linseed-oiled rag:
The stain, a murky brownish yellow.
Don't see a bladder-cancered father's urine.
Don't feel the certain seasick uncertainty
In prognosis, treatment, progressions.
In the way Goya painted the dog.
In the way the pigment of an end looms.
Go into your yellow, the painter says, and so we do.
Nuclear cooling towers overflowing their basin of sunflower fields.

13.

Whatever the season, the dog sees autumn and winter, mostly. Violet, indigo, blue. Yellow, yellow, yellow. Some red. She sees better at night than we because her eyes have more rods, and a reflective surface behind the retina that ricochets light back through. Her *tapetum lucidum*: beautiful tapestry. That's why dogs' eyes shine yellow in the shadows beyond the fire beyond the cave in the darkness our eyes clutch at, pleading for scraps of vision, of understanding, of mercy.

14.

Because it isn't fair,
This pigment, or this yellow.
Because, as we were saying:
We want to know who and what
And where and when and how.
All the way to the beginning.
Why at the heart of every large galaxy
There's a massive black hole.
Dog scratching at the back door.

15.

Strange matter, a dog, warm and panting. Slurry of black fur snuffing dung and death and dirt. The way she bounds through the fields, chasing what we've thrown. Explorer, emissary, inventor, strong force withstanding extreme heat and colossal density. Plunging into the yolk, the very birth pangs of the cosmos. Because we've asked her to.

Now We See

—On Michael Stringer's photograph "Cranefly"

Many months underground or under water,
then a few days skittering through air. The end
of the cranefly's narrative. I've learned that tying
a fly involves wrapping thread around barbules
of wing feather and hackle and then around
and around and around and around and around
before sealing the head of the hook with a spot
of varnish. But these diatomaceous eyes aren't
so simple. They're not about perceiving what's
going to happen or looking back at the past
but seeing the multi-faceted repetitions hidden/
revealed right here, face to face. Now I see
how it all comes together—the geraniums,
the cranberries, the tincture of leaves, the manure,
the manifold roots and condiments of soil, each
iridescent now a darkly mosaic-ed arrangement,
a bob and weave entomology, that which is cut
into sections, cut into, cut out, cut right and left
right now, threading the needle through the nucleus
of now, the glittering advent of doors to the lunar
eclipse of now, a cell dividing and dividing
and dividing dark from light, the what's there
compounded precisely beyond our strangest dreams,
confounding the senses as the lively wild browns
this August feed hard on cranefly and sedge.

Inhabiting the Damp Impervious

—Charles Darwin, *The Voyage of the Beagle*

Out of the kayak, I sink to the ankles
in ooze. For a moment my feet
won't budge. I have to think,

I'm not being swallowed. But I am
shackled. It's not a bad place for it,
these clay banks with kingfishers

chattering, eastern sliders sunning
on tree snags. In fact, it could be nice
to root here by the river, linked

to cycles of day, season, year,
petrifying into scenery. Nothing
vocal or belligerent. Just weather

and chemical interaction.
The truth is, I've become fond
of the tank car in the river.

flood debris squatting offshore,
two decades safety hazard, eyesore,
railroad renegade. I can't help seeing

a creature there, if only the creature
of industry. Maybe it's the quaint
proclamation stenciled

on the barrel-chested drum:
"PURE SWEET MOLASSES."
I have to admire the bravado,

this hollow gong, contents long
gone in a plume of drainage. Still,
what sweetness given to fish,

along with chemicals and petroleum
byproducts. At last, the necessary
offices and departments have conferred:

tomorrow the tank car will be salvaged.
The fish, nobody asked them.
We think fish have nothing to say

about projects or molasses, although
some trains can articulate, if by that we
mean bend. Is that what we are

then? The species with the articulate
tongue? A limb freakishly double-jointed
in ways useless for catching flies or

finding our way or cleaning ourselves
or our young. But a taste for sweetness
is shared by many creatures, including

all hominids. A menagerie craving
that first sugary tear at the seams,
the tank giving out, then giving

way to nonnegotiable forces—
birth, berth, dearth, death, all
spurious fluids; now to be

cranked up by crane, wrenched
from river muck, come to an end
again. Steel intention reduced

to sluice—but surprisingly little
rust, you see, because molasses
is a chelating agent. Dearly

Beloved, only in viscosity
shall we comprehend what is
resurrected, what is preserved.

Notes

"An Entangled Bank" riffs off of and rewrites portions of the last paragraph of Darwin's *On the Origin of Species* and "Spring" in Thoreau's *Walden*, as well as CSO (Combined Sewer Overflow) documents on the City of Lynchburg website.

"Potters' Field" was inspired by a 1994 wind storm in Lynchburg, Virginia, that uprooted trees along the cemetery's perimeter, revealing a potters' field no one had known was there.

The title "*Lares et Penates*" translates as "gods of the household and gods of the crossroads." "*The arch* [. . .] *is nothing else . . .*" is adapted from the *Notebooks* of Leonardo di Vinci, Vol. II. "When these forces . . ." is adapted from *The Ten Books of Architecture* by Leon Battista Alberti. "Above all an arch . . ." is adapted from the writings of Louis Kahn.

"Phosphenes and Entopics" are the spots and patterns of color seen when after pressing on the eyes or receiving a blow to the head.

Portions of the story and language in "*Hóang-Tsong* (The Yellow Bell)" are adapted from Chao-Mei-Pa's *The Yellow Bell: A Brief Sketch of the History of Chinese Music* (Baltimore: Banbury Hill, 1934).

"Mozart's Starling" is the title of a paper by Meredith J. West and Andrew P. King, which was published in *American Scientist*, March-April 1990. Some of the information in the poem is derived from that article.

A number of the poems in this book, including "Meet Me at the Speed of Light" and "Goya's Dog," derive inspiration and adapt words from articles on *Science Daily* (ScienceDaily.com).

Acknowledgments

Thank you to the publications in which these poems first appeared, some in slightly different form:

Blackbird: "Beggars," "Ring-necks"
From the Fishouse: "Doorstep Ecologist," "Phosphenes and Entopics"
The Greensboro Review: "The Brücke Choir," "Crow Psalms"
Gargoyle: "Crowd Looking at a Tied-Up Object," "Meet Me at the Speed of Light," "Recreation Center"
Hawk & Handsaw: "An Entangled Bank"
The Human Genre Project: "Meet Me at the Speed of Light," "Primate Center, Duke University"
ISLE: "Primate Center, Duke University," "On the Ladder"
Isotope: A Journal of Literary Nature and Science Writing: "First Lessons in Beekeeping"
The Louisville Review: "Breaking and Entering"
Many Mountains Moving: "Hôang Tsong (the Yellow Bell)"
Meridian: "Matriarch"
New Virginia Review: "The Art of Navigation"
The Notre Dame Review: "Harmonicas," "Potters' Field"
Poetry Daily: "Matriarch"
Poet Lore: "The Way War Ends"
The Roanoke Review: "Walking the Train Trestle"
Shenandoah: "Lares et Penates"
Terrain.org: A Journal of the Built and Natural Environments: "Goya's Dog"

"Doorstep Ecologist" also appears in *From the Fishouse: An Anthology of Poems that Sing, Rhyme, Resound, Syncopate, Alliterate, and Just Plain Sound Great*, ed. Camille Dungy, Matt O'Donnell, Gerald Stern, and Jeffrey Thomson (Persea Books, 2009).

"Endosymbiosis" was originally commissioned by the New York Festival of Song.

"An Entangled Bank" also appears in *The Ecopoetry Anthology*, ed. Ann Fisher-Wirth and Laura-Gray Street (Trinity University Press, 2013).

"Goya's Dog" also appears in *Dogs Singing: A Tribute Anthology*, ed. Jessie Lendennie (Salmon Poetry, 2010)

"Ring-necks" was chosen by George Garrett to appear in *Best New Poets 2005*, ed. George Garrett and Jeb Livingood (Samover Press and Meridian, 2005).

Many, many thanks to the teachers, friends, and organizations who through the years have helped me to write and rewrite these poems: Debra Allbery, Karen Brennan, Claudia Emerson, Ann Fisher-Wirth, Bunny Goodjohn, Jay Kardan, Jeanne Larson, Larry Levis, Elizabeth Seydel Morgan, Jim Peterson, Ira Sadoff, Bill and Sydna Street, Carole Weinstein, Christian Wiman, the Virginia Center for Creative Arts, the Virginia Commission for the Arts, the Artist House at St. Mary's College of Maryland, and all my colleagues in the English Department at Randolph College

Photo: Dave Blount

LAURA-GRAY STREET is co-editor of *The Ecopoetry Anthology* (Trinity University Press, 2013) and has been the recipient of poetry prizes from *The Greensboro Review*, the Dana Awards, the Southern Women Writers Conference, *Isotope: A Journal of Literary Science and Nature Writing*, and *Terrain.org: A Journal of the Built and Natural Environments*. Her work has been published in *Poet Lore, ISLE, Shenandoah, Blackbird, The Notre Dame Review*, and elsewhere; and supported by fellowships from the Virginia Commission for the Arts, the Virginia Center for the Creative Arts, and the Artist House at St. Mary's College in Maryland. She teaches at Randolph College in Lynchburg, Virginia.